The Big Book o

SPACE

David Glover

Created and published by
Two-Can Publishing
43-45 Dorset Street
London W1U 7NA

Copyright © 2002 Two-Can Publishing

All rights reserved. No part of this publication may be reproduced, stored in a retrieval system or transmitted in any form or by any means electronic, mechanical, photocopying, recording or otherwise, without written permission of the copyright owner.

'Two-Can' is a trademark of Two-Can Publishing.
Two-Can Publishing is a division of
Zenith Entertainment Ltd
43-45 Dorset Street
London W1U 7NA

SC ISBN 1-84301-018-6

Dewey Decimal Classification 523.1

SC 10 9 8 7 6 5 4 3 2 1

A catalogue record for this book is available from the British Library.

Printed and bound in Spain by Graficas Reunidas

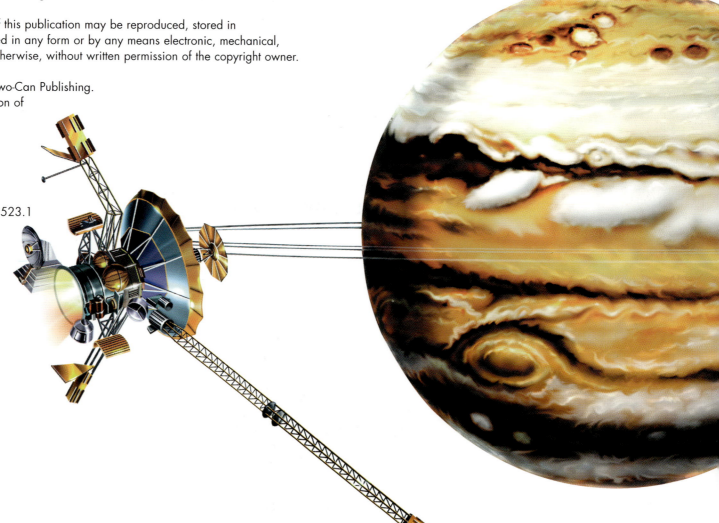

Author: David Glover
Consultant: Carole Stott FRAS
Main illustrations: Bob Corley (Artist Partners Ltd),
Duncan Gutteridge (Artist Partners Ltd), Gary Bines (Blue Chip Illustration)
Small illustrations: Phillip Morrison, Mel Pickering

Photographic credits:
Bob Gathany/Dorling Kindersley p31 (t); Dorling Kindersley courtesy of The Science Museum p30; Frank Spooner Pictures p44; NASA p5, p11, p14, p17, p18, p19, p26, p27 (b), p32, p35, p39 (t & b), p40; Planet Earth Pictures p12, p20, p33; Science Photo Library p7, p8, p21, p25, p27 (t), p28, p29, p31 (b), p43; Tony Stone Images p13.

Contents

What is space? 4
Our solar system 6
Sun 8
Mercury and Venus 10
Earth and Moon 12
Mars 14
Jupiter and Saturn 16
Uranus, Neptune and Pluto 18
Comet, meteoroid and asteroid 20
Star 22
Constellations 24
Galaxy 26
Astronomy 28
Telescope 30
Space traveller 32
Rocket 34
Space shuttle 36
Space station 38
Space probe 40
Satellite 42
Into the future 44
Glossary 46
Index 48

Words that appear in **bold** in the text are explained in the glossary.

What is space?

On a clear night, when you look at the **stars**, you are looking deep into space. These stars, together with **billions** more that you cannot see, are grouped together in vast star cities, called **galaxies**. Among the stars, there are clouds of glowing **gas** called **nebulae**. These objects and many more, including spinning **planets**, rocky **moons** and **black holes**, make up the **universe**.

▼ **The universe**
The universe contains everything that exists, from tiny specks of dust to vast galaxies that are made of billions of stars.

stars

galaxies

▼ **Big Bang**
Most scientists believe that all the material in the universe was created by a huge explosion called the **Big Bang**. This is how they think it happened.

About 15 billion years ago, in less than a second, a fireball burst into existence. Just after the Big Bang, everything flew apart at high speed. This is how the universe began.

Ten billion years ago, as the universe began to cool down, gas and dust clumped together to form clouds. These clouds became galaxies and stars.

Five billion years ago, a star, our Sun, formed at the centre of a gas cloud. Leftover parts of the cloud created nine planets. These make up part of our **solar system**.

Four billion years ago, our home, planet Earth, began to cool down. Land, oceans and the **atmosphere**, which is a thin blanket of gases around the Earth, began to form.

nebulae

Space exploration ▶
Hubble is a **telescope** that was launched into space by a **space shuttle**. It takes pictures of distant galaxies which help us to unravel the mysteries of space.

stars

planet Jupiter

planet Saturn

Looking into the past
Distances in space are so huge that they are measured by how far light travels in one year. This is called a **light year**. One light year is 9.5 million million kilometres (5.9 million million miles). There is a star called Rigel which is about 900 light years away from Earth. It's hard to imagine, but when you look at this star, you are looking back in time. The light you see today left Rigel more than 900 years before you were born!

Three billion years ago, the first living things appeared. They were simple animals called bacteria. Three million years later, jellyfish and plants appeared in the oceans.

Two million years ago, the first humans walked upright on two legs. They discovered how to make tools, to use fire and, eventually, how to talk, to write and to build machines.

Our solar system

The Earth is one of nine **planets** that travel round, or **orbit**, the fiery **star** we call the **Sun**. The speeding planets and our bright Sun belong to a huge family called the **solar system**. More than 60 **moons** and dark lumps of rock, known as **asteroids**, are also part of the solar system. A thick band of asteroids circles the Sun like a loose belt.

Gravity and orbits

The planets are held in their orbits by **gravity**, which is a special force that pulls objects together. Gravity pulls on the planets in the same way that a string pulls on a toy plane when you whirl it in a circle. Gravity acts everywhere in the **universe**. It keeps the stars in their **galaxies** and pulls you firmly to the ground. Without gravity, you would just float away from the Earth into space.

Pluto

▼ **Our solar system**
This picture shows the order in which the planets orbit the Sun.

Neptune

Uranus

ISAAC NEWTON DISCOVERS GRAVITY

According to a story, about 300 years ago, the English scientist Isaac Newton was sitting under a tree. An apple fell from the tree and hit him on the head. Newton realized that gravity had pulled the apple to Earth.

Newton's discovery made him think about lots of other things. He realized that gravity keeps the Moon orbiting the Earth. Gravity also keeps all the planets travelling in their orbits round the Sun.

WOW!
The Sun's light reaches Earth in 8 minutes, but it would take you 170 years to reach the Sun in a family car!

Planets

The nine planets in our solar system all travel round the Sun in the same direction, but each one takes a different amount of time to complete a full orbit. The time it takes a planet to travel round the Sun once is called the planet's year. As each planet orbits the Sun, it also spins like a top. The time it takes a planet to spin round once is called the planet's day.

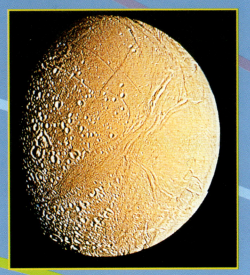

Moons

A moon is a rocky ball that orbits a planet. Some moons are tiny and others are large, but each moon is smaller than the planet it orbits. All the planets, apart from Mercury and Venus, have one or more moons. The Earth has one moon.

◀ **Frozen moon**
Enceladus is one of Saturn's moons. It has a hard, frozen surface.

Sun

The **Sun** is a **star**. It is a giant, bubbling ball of **gas** that gives out huge amounts of heat and light. It is our nearest star and is so big that you could fit more than one million Earths inside it. The Sun's warm rays of light shine down through the Earth's **atmosphere**, providing **energy** for life on our **planet**. The Sun is about half-way through its life, but don't worry – it will keep on shining for **billions** of years!

▼ **The Sun**
This picture shows the Sun's surface and what happens inside the Sun.

Sunspots
These dark, cooler patches, known as sunspots, appear on the Sun's surface.

▲ **Setting Sun**
During the day, the Sun glows like a brilliant ball, but in the evening, it looks dimmer and it seems to sink in the sky.

How sunlight affects the Earth

Imagine the Earth without sunlight. It would be a lifeless ball of rock with no animals or people, and no summer or winter. Sunlight warms the land, oceans and atmosphere. It heats the air, making winds blow and rain fall. Plants need the energy from sunlight to grow, making food for animals, which includes you. Every single second, Earth receives more energy from the Sun than all the power stations on Earth can make in a day.

SUN PROFILE

Age
5 billion years

Composition
Glowing ball of boiling hot gases, including hydrogen and helium

Distance from Earth
150 million km
(93 million mls)

Surface temperature
6,000 °C (10,768 °F)

Temperature at centre
15 million °C (27 million °F)

Core
The Sun's boiling centre, or core, is like an engine room. This is where the Sun makes its energy.

Convective zone
Pockets of energy rise up from the core to this area, called the convective zone.

Photosphere
The photosphere is the part of the Sun you can see. Energy escapes as heat and light from here.

SOLAR ECLIPSE

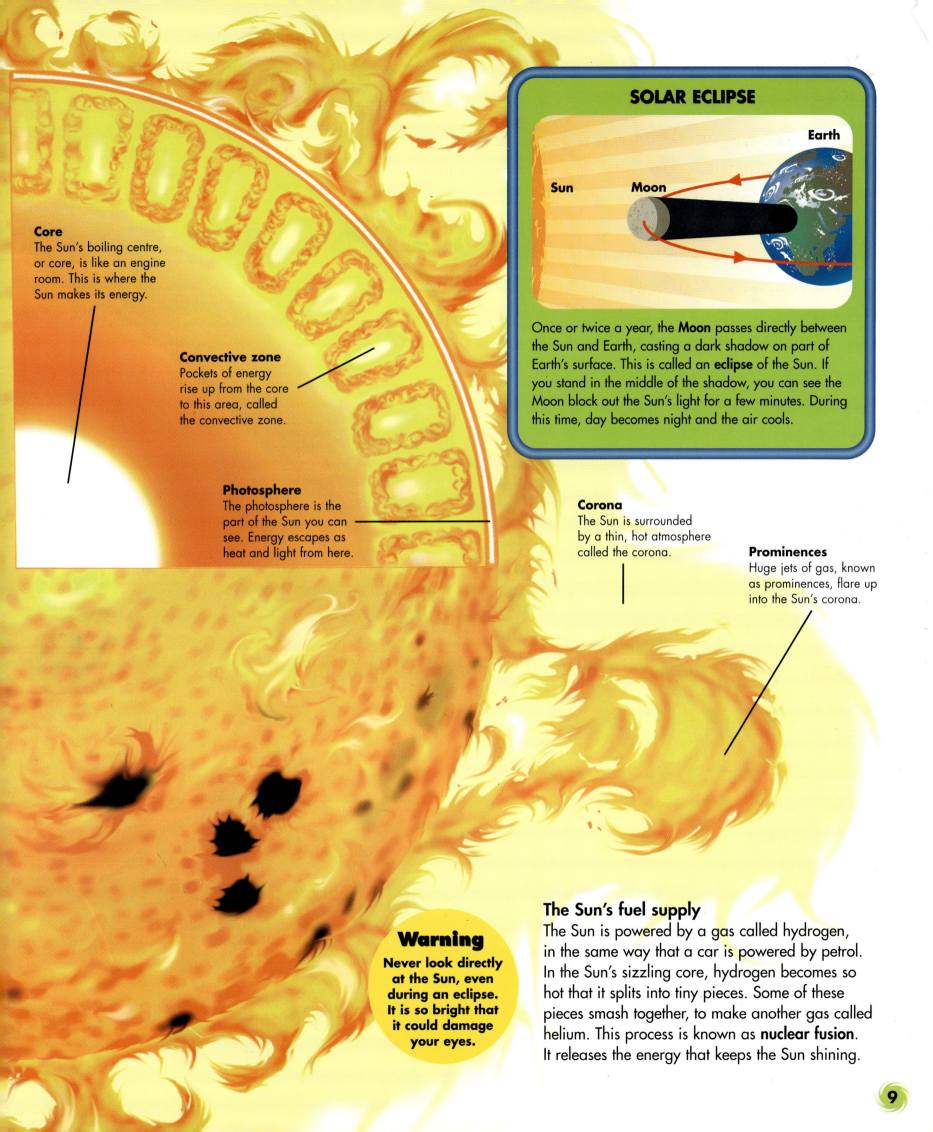

Once or twice a year, the **Moon** passes directly between the Sun and Earth, casting a dark shadow on part of Earth's surface. This is called an **eclipse** of the Sun. If you stand in the middle of the shadow, you can see the Moon block out the Sun's light for a few minutes. During this time, day becomes night and the air cools.

Corona
The Sun is surrounded by a thin, hot atmosphere called the corona.

Prominences
Huge jets of gas, known as prominences, flare up into the Sun's corona.

Warning
Never look directly at the Sun, even during an eclipse. It is so bright that it could damage your eyes.

The Sun's fuel supply
The Sun is powered by a gas called hydrogen, in the same way that a car is powered by petrol. In the Sun's sizzling core, hydrogen becomes so hot that it splits into tiny pieces. Some of these pieces smash together, to make another gas called helium. This process is known as **nuclear fusion**. It releases the energy that keeps the Sun shining.

Mercury and Venus

Mercury and Venus are the closest **planets** to the **Sun**. They are also the hottest of all the planets. Like many other planets, Mercury and Venus are named after characters from ancient Greek and Roman stories. Mercury takes its name from a quick-footed Roman messenger because it races round the Sun in only 88 days. Venus is named after the Roman goddess of love and beauty. It shines brightly in the night sky.

MERCURY PROFILE

Composition	Iron and nickel core with a rocky crust
Special features	Surface craters, no **atmosphere**
Number of moons	0
Distance from Sun	58 million km (36 million mls)
Orbit	88 Earth days
Temperature	-170 °C to 430 °C (-274 °F to 806 °F)

Mercury

Mercury is a lifeless ball, less than half the size of Earth. If you stood on Mercury, the Sun would look nearly three times bigger than it does from Earth. It would feel nearly five times as hot. As Mercury spins in and out of the Sun's light, its temperature changes dramatically. The side of Mercury that faces the Sun is hotter than a roaring coal fire but the side that faces away is colder than ice.

Caloris Basin

A GIANT CRATER

Mercury's surface is covered with thousands of hollows in the ground called **craters**. These are made by pieces of rock crashing into the surface. Mercury's largest crater, the Caloris Basin, is 1,300 kilometres (808 miles) across. It would take almost one day for a bus to travel from one side of the crater to the other.

Venus

From Earth, Venus glows brightly in the night sky, but close up the planet is a deathly, scorching inferno. Venus is covered by thick, poisonous yellow clouds. Its atmosphere presses down so hard that it would crush your body immediately. Only specially designed spacecraft can survive on Venus – and then just for a short time.

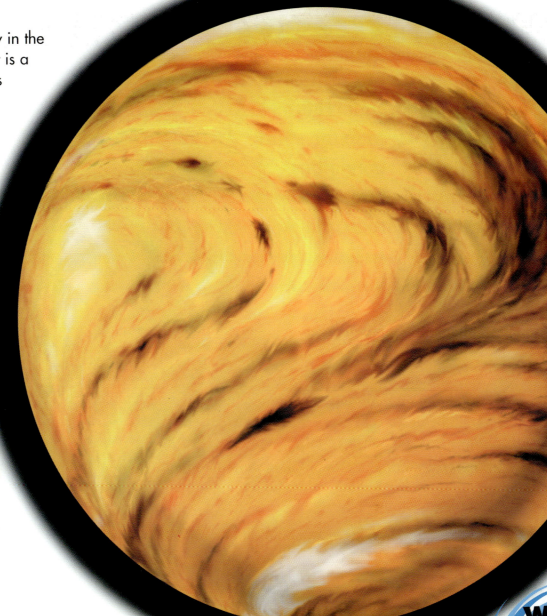

VENUS PROFILE	
Composition	
Iron core with a rocky crust	
Special features	
Poisonous atmosphere of **gas** clouds covering a rocky surface	
Number of moons	
0	
Distance from Sun	
108 million km (67 million mls)	
Orbit	
224 Earth days	
Temperature	
Up to 460 °C (860 °F)	

WOW! Avoid Venus because you'll be roasted in seconds. It's the hottest planet in our solar system.

Below the clouds

Venus is about the same size as Earth and is also Earth's next-door neighbour. For a long time, **astronomers** thought that Venus was Earth's twin and that, like Earth, it was a cool world covered with watery oceans. But visiting spacecraft discovered that beneath the planet's clouds, Venus is a baking, dry desert. In some places, the flat ground rises into high **volcanoes** and jagged mountains.

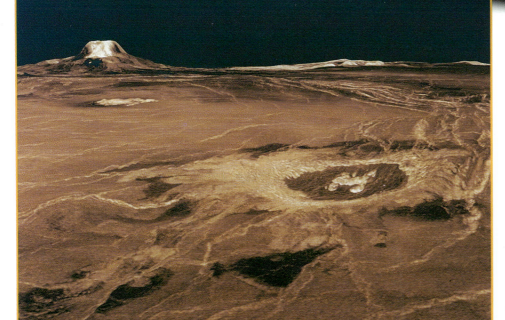

◀ **Magellan**
In 1990, the **space probe** Magellan orbited Venus. Special cameras that 'saw' beneath the deadly clouds showed deep craters dotted on the planet's surface.

Earth and Moon

Our home, **planet** Earth, is the third planet from the **Sun**. This makes it perfectly placed in the **solar system** to create the right conditions for life. Earth is neither too hot nor too cold. There is fresh air, warmth and plenty of running water for plants and animals to survive. The **Moon**, which **orbits** the Earth, is a dry, rocky ball. It has no **atmosphere** and no life.

Earth
At the centre of the Earth, there is a core of solid metal, surrounded by layers of liquid metal and rock. The outer layer of rock is called the crust. Running water covers three-quarters of the crust. The atmosphere surrounding the Earth is called the air. It contains the **gas** oxygen, which you need to breathe.

▼ **Earth's features**
Planet Earth's crust is crinkled with deep valleys and high mountains.

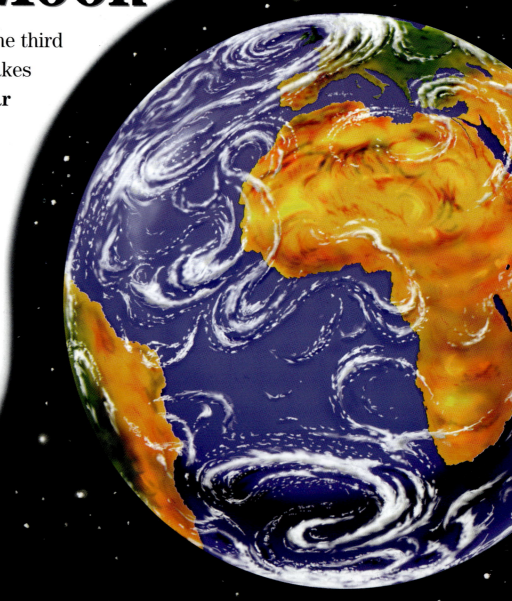

Night and day
As Earth orbits the Sun, it spins round. When one side of Earth faces the Sun, it is daytime. When it faces away from the Sun, it is night-time.

▶ **The Earth and Moon**
This picture shows how the Earth would look from the Moon. You would see clearly Earth's swirling clouds and deep blue oceans.

EARTH PROFILE
Composition
Iron and nickel core with a rocky crust
Special features
Running water and animal and plant life
Number of moons
1
Distance from Sun
150 million km (93 million mls)
Orbit
365.25 Earth days
Temperature
-70 °C to 55 °C (-94 °F to 131 °F)

The Moon

Apart from the Sun, the Moon is the brightest object in the sky. But the Moon does not give out light. The brightness you see is light reflected from the Sun. If you look at the Moon through a pair of binoculars, you can see that its surface is pitted with rugged **craters** and high mountain ridges. The craters formed **billions** of years ago, when rocky objects, such as **asteroids**, crashed through space and collided violently with the Moon. Nothing lives on the barren Moon, but twelve humans have walked on its surface.

▲ **Moon in the sky**
The side of the Moon facing the Sun is blazing hot. The opposite side is freezing cold.

THE MOON'S PHASES

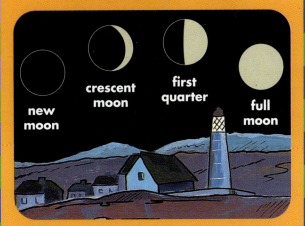

new moon · crescent moon · first quarter · full moon

The Moon seems to change its shape in the sky. This is because we see different parts of its sunlit side as it orbits the Earth. Sometimes the Moon seems to disappear completely. At other times, it looks like a thin crescent. When the Moon is full, it looks like a bright disk. These changes are called the phases of the Moon.

MOON PROFILE
Composition
Rock, possibly with a small metal core
Special features
No atmosphere, wind or weather
Distance from Earth
384,000 km (239,000 mls)
Orbit round Earth
27.3 Earth days
Temperature
-170 °C to 110 °C (-274 °F to 230 °F)

Mars

Mars is the fourth **planet** from the **Sun** and just over half the size of Earth. Long ago, Mars may have been a watery world but today it is barren and dry. Its landscape is dotted with deep **craters** and huge **volcanoes**. Mars will probably be the next planet that humans visit. But they will need special equipment to help them breathe and thick, warm clothes to protect them against the ice-cold air.

The red planet
It's easy to tell whether you are standing on Mars or on Earth. On Earth the sky is blue, but on Mars it is pink. This is because the surface of Mars is covered with a fine, rust-coloured dust that is whipped into the air by violent summer storms. From Earth, this dust makes Mars look red in the night sky, so Mars is often called the 'red planet'.

▲ **Desolate desert**
The surface of Mars, with its dry, sandy ground and jagged rocks, is similar to some of the deserts you find on Earth.

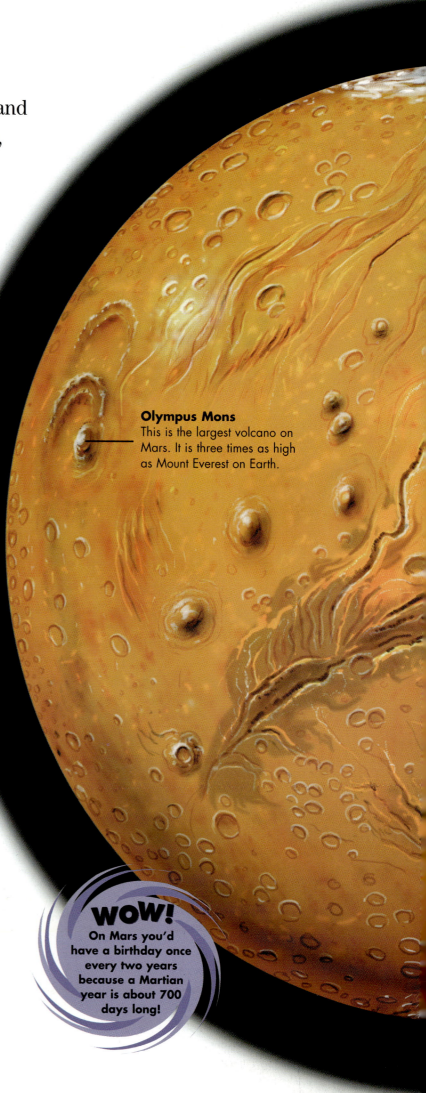

Olympus Mons
This is the largest volcano on Mars. It is three times as high as Mount Everest on Earth.

WOW!
On Mars you'd have a birthday once every two years because a Martian year is about 700 days long!

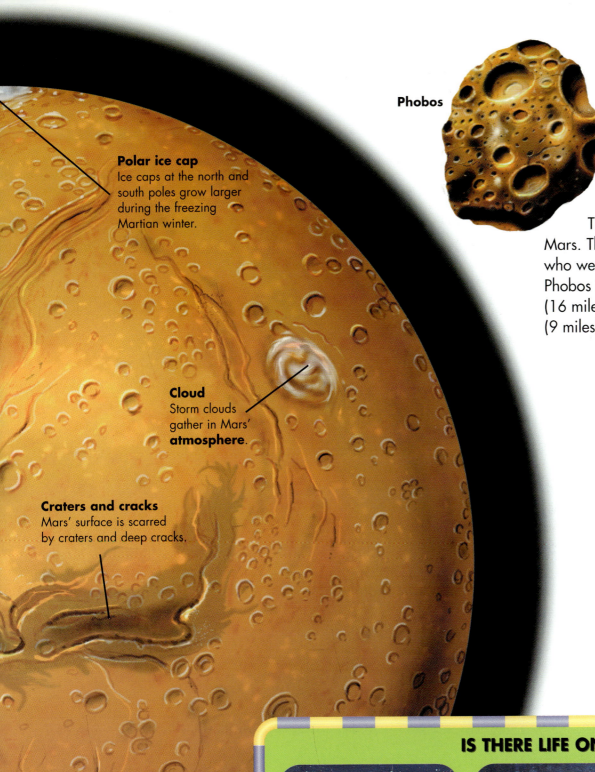

Polar ice cap
Ice caps at the north and south poles grow larger during the freezing Martian winter.

Cloud
Storm clouds gather in Mars' **atmosphere**.

Craters and cracks
Mars' surface is scarred by craters and deep cracks.

Polar ice cap

Phobos   Deimos

Phobos and Deimos
These two potato-shaped **moons orbit** Mars. They are named after Phobos and Deimos, who were the sons of the Roman god Mars. Phobos is a lump of rock about 26 kilometres (16 miles) long. Deimos is just 14 kilometres (9 miles) long – the length of 132 football pitches.

MARS PROFILE
Composition
Iron core, rocky surface with ice in the far north and south

Special features
Rusty red soil

Number of moons
2

Distance from Sun
228 million km (142 million mls)

Orbit
1.88 Earth years

Temperature
-120 °C to 25 °C (-185 °F to 77 °F)

IS THERE LIFE ON MARS?

One hundred years ago, **astronomers** studied Mars through **telescopes**. They thought they saw evidence of running water on Mars' surface.

In 1976, the Viking Lander spacecraft landed on Mars. It tested the soil, but found no signs of water. Astronomers decided that there was no life on Mars.

A few scientists think there may be tiny life forms on Mars. In the future, other spacecraft will land on the planet. Perhaps then, we will find out for sure.

Jupiter and Saturn

Jupiter and Saturn are the biggest **planets** in our **solar system**. They are giant balls of brightly coloured swirling **gas**. If you tried to land a spacecraft on Jupiter or Saturn, it would just sink into thick, soupy clouds. Both planets spin round incredibly quickly, which makes them bulge in the middle.

Jupiter

In ancient Roman stories, Jupiter was the king of the gods. The planet Jupiter is the king of the planets. It is so large that all the other planets in our solar system could fit into it. At Jupiter's centre, hidden far beneath the clouds, there is a solid rock-and-metal core.

JUPITER PROFILE

Composition
Gas, liquid and metal with a solid core

Special features
Largest planet, red and yellow clouds and the Great Red Spot

Number of moons
At least 16

Distance from Sun
777 million km (483 million mls)

Orbit
11.86 Earth years

Cloud-top temperature
-120 °C (-184 °F)

Great Red Spot
This giant storm, called the Great Red Spot, has been raging for more than 300 years.

Jupiter's moons

Jupiter is millions of miles away, but on a clear night, with a pair of binoculars, you can see Jupiter's four largest **moons**. Io is covered with a red-and-yellow gas and Europa is a small frozen world. Ganymede and Callisto are made from ice and rock.

Io   Europa   Ganymede   Callisto

Saturn

Saturn is named after the Roman god of agriculture. Like Jupiter, Saturn is made up mostly of gas and liquids, with a rocky core. About every thirty years, fierce winds whip violently around Saturn. They churn up the surface, making white storms appear in the clouds.

Voyager
In the 1980s, the Voyager spacecraft flew past Saturn and sent back detailed pictures of the planet's rings.

WOW! Saturn is light enough to float in water – if you could find a bowl big enough!

Saturn's rings

Thousands of beautifully coloured rings spin round Saturn. Each ring is made up of **billions** of pieces of icy rock. Some of the pieces are huge chunks, while others are tiny flecks, almost too small to see. Together, the rings are nearly ten times as wide as the Earth, but only 1.6 kilometres (1 mile) high. Jupiter, Uranus and Neptune also have rings, but they are not as spectacular as Saturn's.

▲ **A view from Voyager**
Voyager took several close-up pictures of Saturn's bright rings.

SATURN PROFILE

Composition
Gas and liquid with a rocky core

Special features
Colourful rings

Number of moons
At least 18

Distance from Sun
1.4 billion km (870 million mls)

Orbit
29.5 Earth years

Cloud-top temperature
-120 °C (-184 °F)

Uranus, Neptune and Pluto

By the 1700s, **astronomers** had spotted six **planets**. The other three, Uranus, Neptune and Pluto, the most distant planets from the **Sun**, were discovered when astronomers searched the sky with powerful **telescopes**. Uranus and Neptune are green and blue **gas** giants. Lonely Pluto is a small, cold ball of rock and ice.

WOW!
Neptune and Uranus are brightly coloured because light is reflected by the poisonous gas in their clouds.

URANUS PROFILE
Composition
Gas with a rocky core
Special features
Spins on its side
Number of moons
17
Distance from Sun
3 **billion** km (1.8 billion mls)
Orbit
84 Earth years
Cloud-top temperature
-210 °C (-346 °F)

Uranus
In 1781, Uranus was spotted by the astronomer William Herschel. It was the first new planet to be discovered since ancient times and was named after the god of the sky in Greek and Roman mythology. Uranus has a rocky core which is covered with layers of gas. Unlike the other planets, which spin like tops, Uranus lies on its side and spins more like a wheel.

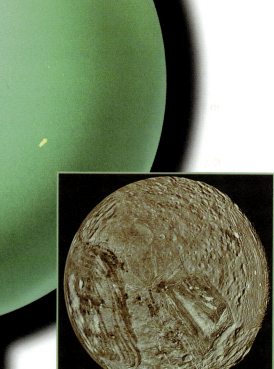

▲ **Miranda**
Miranda is one of Uranus' **moons**. Deep, jagged grooves mark its surface.

Neptune

Neptune is named after the Roman god of the sea. It has a small rocky core covered with thick gases that reflect a bluish light. When the **space probe** Voyager 2 flew past Neptune, it discovered a huge dark storm cloud the same size as Earth. Scientists call it the Great Dark Spot. Here, winds blow four times faster than the most powerful storm on Earth.

Great Dark Spot

NEPTUNE PROFILE

Composition
Gas and ice with a small rocky core

Special features
Storm cloud, the Great Dark Spot, blowing at 2,000 km (1,243 mls) per hour

Number of moons
8

Distance from Sun
4.5 billion km (2.8 billion mls)

Orbit
164.79 Earth years

Cloud-top temperature
-210 °C (-346 °F)

◀ **Triton**
Neptune's largest moon is called Triton. It is probably the coldest place in the solar system.

PLUTO PROFILE

Composition
Icy surface with a rocky core

Special features
Smallest and furthest planet in the **solar system**

Number of moons
1

Distance from Sun
5.9 billion km (3.7 billion mls)

Orbit
248 Earth years

Cloud-top temperature
-210 °C (-346 °F)

Charon

Pluto

Pluto

Pluto is named after the Greek god of the Underworld. It is the smallest planet and is furthest from the Sun. Pluto's path round the Sun sometimes takes it inside Neptune's **orbit**. For a short time, this means that Neptune is the furthest planet from the Sun. Pluto has one icy moon called Charon.

Comet, meteoroid and asteroid

Have you ever spotted sudden flashes of light, or a tail of light, streaming across the night sky? These spectacular light shows are made by rocks from space, called **meteoroids**, that burn up in the Earth's **atmosphere**. Other kinds of space rocks, such as **comets** and **asteroids**, can also be seen in the sky. All of these rocks **orbit** the **Sun**.

Comet
A comet is an enormous, dirty snowball that is made of snow, ice and rock. When a comet's orbit takes it close to the Sun, the Sun's heat melts some of the ice. This creates a hazy cloud millions of kilometres long, that looks like a gigantic tail.

Comet's tail
This always points away from the Sun.

Regular arrivals
A comet follows a long, **elliptical** orbit. Some comets take thousands of years to orbit the Sun. Others, such as Halley's comet, appear more frequently. Each time a comet repeats an orbit, it becomes smaller and smaller until finally, it disappears completely.

▼ **Halley's comet**
In 1705, the **astronomer** Edmond Halley calculated correctly that the comet he saw in the night sky would return every 76 years.

Comet's head
This always points towards the Sun.

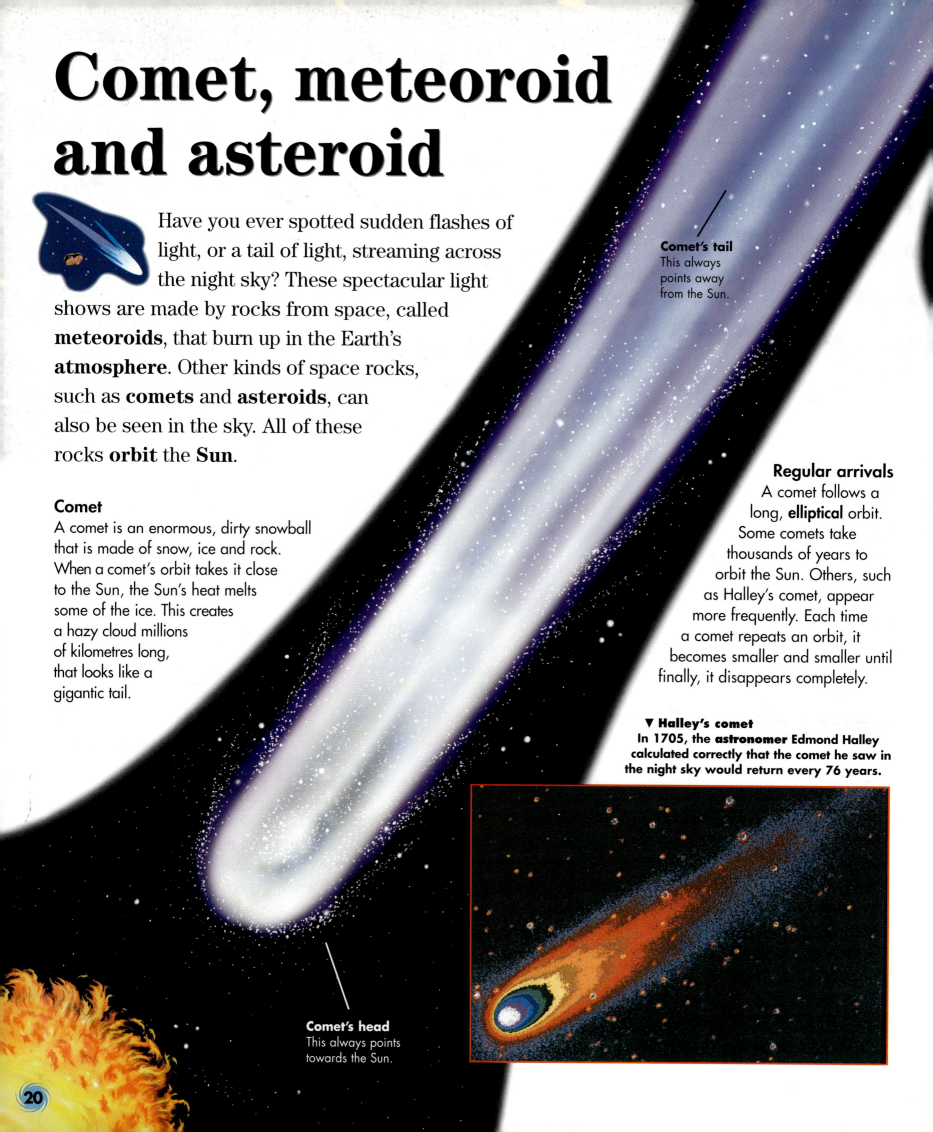

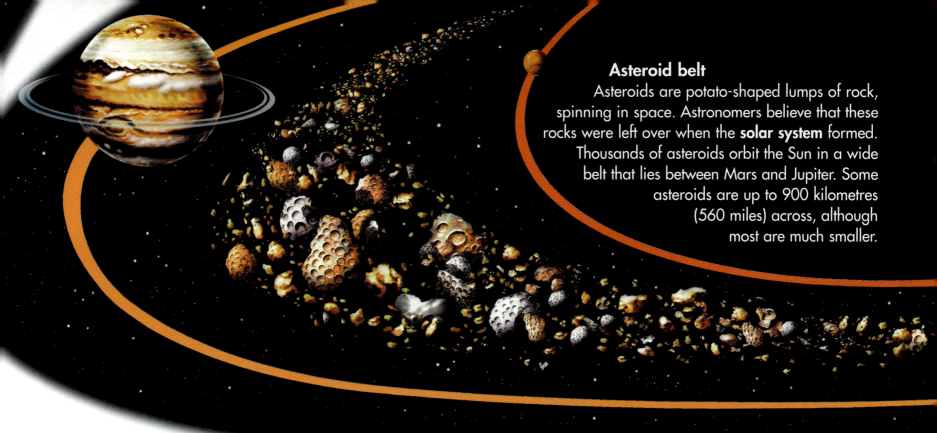

Asteroid belt
Asteroids are potato-shaped lumps of rock, spinning in space. Astronomers believe that these rocks were left over when the **solar system** formed. Thousands of asteroids orbit the Sun in a wide belt that lies between Mars and Jupiter. Some asteroids are up to 900 kilometres (560 miles) across, although most are much smaller.

Meteoroids
Meteoroids are rough lumps of dust, rock and metal that fly through space between the **planets**. They are fragments of large comets and asteroids. You cannot see a meteoroid high up in space, but you may be able to spot it when it falls through space and whizzes into the Earth's atmosphere.

FROM METEOROID TO METEORITE

Many millions of meteoroids swarm through space. Most meteoroids are the size of pebbles, but a few can be bigger than a skyscraper.

When a meteoroid enters Earth's atmosphere, it usually burns up in a flash, leaving a bright trail in the sky. It is now called a meteor or a shooting star.

A meteoroid can fall through the Earth's atmosphere without burning up completely. When it eventually crashes into Earth, it is called a meteorite.

Falling to Earth
Every year, millions of meteoroids fall to Earth. Most land as harmless specks of dust. Each day, space dust weighing twice as much as the Statue of Liberty floats gently to Earth. Many scientists believe that, millions of years ago, a huge meteorite crashed into Earth and churned up so much dust that it blocked out the Sun's light. Without light, the dinosaurs and other animals died.

◀ **Arizona**
This **crater** in Arizona, USA, is nearly 1.6 kilometres (1 mile) across. It was made about 25,000 years ago by an enormous meteorite.

Star

A **star** is a gigantic ball of glowing **gas**. It is born from space dust, burns for **billions** of years, then becomes dust again. The night sky is dotted with billions of stars that look like pinpricks of light in the distance. But only one star, the **Sun**, is close enough for you to feel its heat and to see it as a glowing ball.

STAR PROFILE (SIZE OF THE SUN)
Composition
Hydrogen and helium gas
Special features
Produces heat and light
Colour
Yellow, blue or red
Temperature
from 2,500 °C (4,532 °F) to 45,000 °C (81,032 °F)
Lifespan
About 10 billion years. Our Sun is half-way through its life.

Life and death of a star

A star's life story depends on its **mass**, or the amount of gas it contains. A star that contains a lot of gas burns quickly and has a short life. A star that contains less gas burns slowly and has a longer life. Our Sun has enough gas to keep shining for another five billion years.

▼ The stars
Here you can see two different paths a star's life may take.

Black dwarf
Eventually, a white dwarf cools and ends its life as a **black dwarf**. Now, it is like a burnt-out ball of ash.

White dwarf
As a red giant grows old, it shrinks into a **white dwarf**. It becomes a cold, heavy ball, no bigger than the Earth.

Nebula
A star begins its life in a swirling cloud of dust and gas, called a **nebula**.

Red giant
After millions of years, when a star like our Sun reaches middle age, it begins to swell and to cool down. At this stage, it is called a **red giant**.

A star forms
The dust and gas clump together into a tight ball inside the nebula.

A glowing star
The young star heats up and

Supergiant
This star has a mass about ten times greater than our Sun. When this star enters middle age, it expands into a red or blue **supergiant**.

Supernova
Towards the end of its life, a supergiant explodes in a blaze of light called a **supernova**.

Neutron star
A supernova leaves behind a cloud of dust and gas with a small, but incredibly heavy, centre. This is a **neutron star**. A tiny speck of this star would weigh as much as a house.

DIAMONDS IN THE SKY

Stars twinkle and shine in the sky like diamonds. **Astronomers** believe that they have discovered an old star, the size of Earth, made of solid diamond. This jewel in the sky is 17 **light years** away.

Black hole
Not all supergiants end their lives as neutron stars. When a supergiant explodes into a supernova, **gravity** can pull so hard on the material left at its centre that it collapses into a **black hole**. This is an area of space where gravity is so strong that nothing, not even light, can escape. If you were unlucky enough to fall into a black hole, time would slow down and you would be stretched out like a piece of spaghetti.

23

Constellations

At a glance, **stars** look like random dots of light, but if you study them carefully you will see patterns. These patterns are called **constellations**. **Astronomers** group the stars into 88 constellations. People who live in the northern half of the world see a different part of the sky and different constellations from people who live in the southern half of the world.

WOW! North American Indians tested warriors' eyesight by seeing how many stars they could spot in the night sky!

▼ **Northern constellation stars** These are the constellations that you can see from places such as Europe and North America. Look for the Great Bear and the row of three bright stars in Orion.

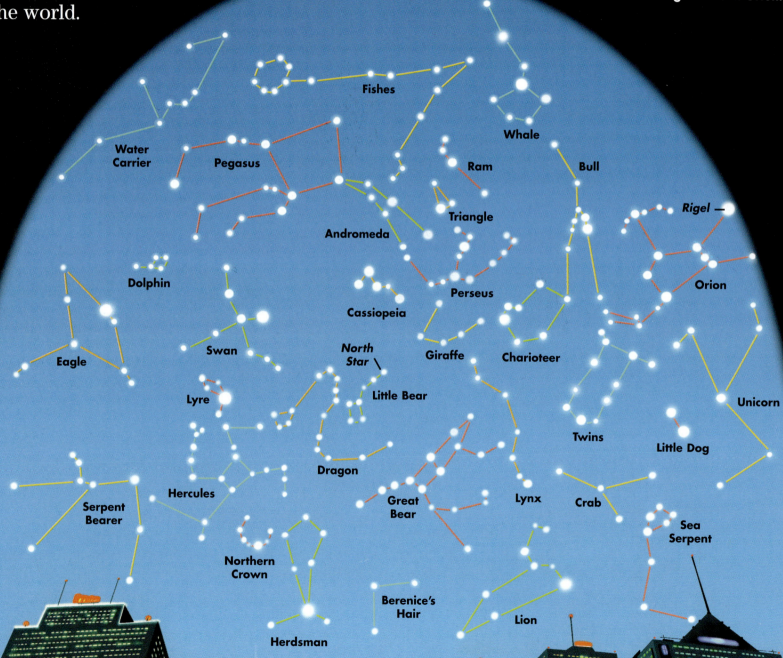

24

Spinning in space

When you look up at the night sky, the stars seem to move. Really, the stars do not move at all. It is the Earth spinning round that makes the stars look as though they are moving. For centuries, sailors have used the stars to work out their position at sea. The North Star shines above the North Pole. By finding the North Star, sailors can tell which way is north and work out the direction in which they are travelling.

▶ **Navigating by the stars**
In the 14th century, sailors measured the position of the stars with a special instrument called an astrolabe.

▼ **Southern constellation stars**
These are the constellations that you can see from places such as Australia and South America. The brightest star, apart from the Sun, is Sirius. It is in the Great Dog constellation.

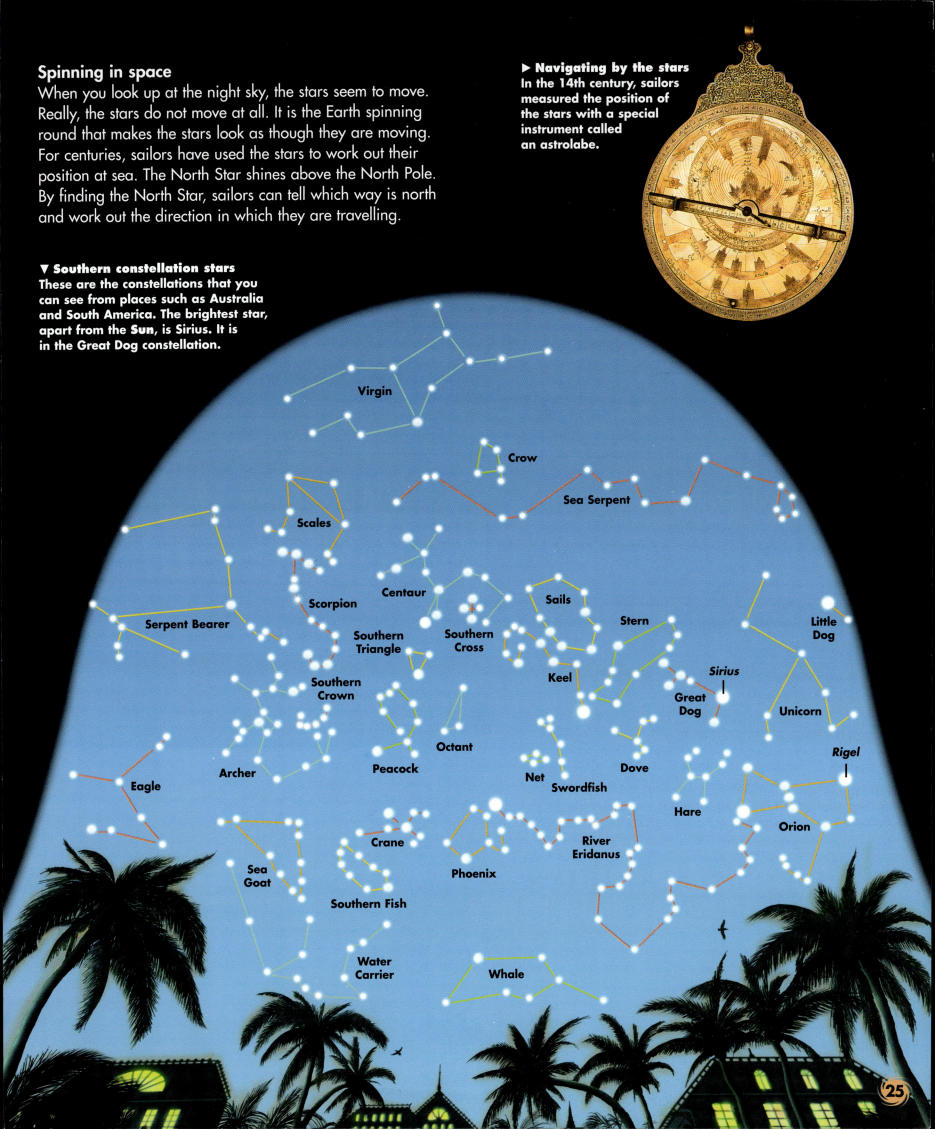

Galaxy

How many **stars** are there, thousands or millions? No, there are **billions** and billions! Stars are clumped together in star cities called **galaxies**. Each galaxy is made up of billions of stars, and there are 100 billion galaxies in the **universe**. The stars you see with your eyes are all in our own galaxy, called the **Milky Way**. Most of the other galaxies are so far away that you can see them only with a **telescope**.

▲ **Deep space**
This photograph of galaxies deep in space was taken with a powerful telescope. The galaxies may look close together, but really they are millions of kilometres apart.

Types of galaxies

Galaxies are all different shapes. A spiral galaxy has long, curved arms that make it look like a spinning firework. A barred spiral galaxy is similar, but it has a bar across the centre. An **elliptical** galaxy is shaped like an egg, while an irregular galaxy has no set shape. Stars and clouds of dust are most concentrated in a galaxy's arms or its bulging centre.

▼ spiral galaxy

▲ barred spiral galaxy

▲ elliptical galaxy

WOW! If you counted all day and all night, it would take you 3,000 years to count all the stars in one galaxy.

Milky Way

The Milky Way is a spiral galaxy that spans 100,000 **light years** from one side to the other. On a dark night, you may be able to see part of the Milky Way. It is a band of billions of stars stretching across the night sky. The **Sun**, which is about 30,000 light years from the centre of the Milky Way, moves round in one of the galaxy's arms.

▶ **Milky Way**
This photograph of the Milky Way was taken on a clear night. When you look at the Milky Way, you can see glittering stars and hazy clouds of dust.

Other galaxies

Astronomers with powerful telescopes have photographed and mapped the positions of millions of galaxies. Astronomers discovered that galaxies are grouped together in clusters. In between the clusters, there is nothing but empty space. The Milky Way belongs to a cluster that includes smaller galaxies called the Magellanic Clouds and the Andromeda Galaxy. You can just make out the Andromeda Galaxy as a smudge of light in the sky. It is the most distant thing in the universe that you can see with the naked eye.

▲ **Andromeda**
The Andromeda Galaxy is over two million light years away from Earth.

A TINY SPECK IN THE UNIVERSE

1 Do you feel small in a big city? In this picture, a city is marked by a red dot. The city is tiny compared with the whole Earth.

2 If planet Earth makes a city seem small, then imagine how small Earth seems within the **solar system**.

3 Can you see our solar system? It is now just a speck on one of the spiral arms of the Milky Way.

4 Even the Milky Way is just a tiny galaxy. It belongs to a group that has about 30 other galaxies.

Astronomy

Since ancient times, people have gazed in wonder at the **Sun**, the **Moon** and the **stars**. **Astronomers** spend their lives studying space. They use **telescopes** and other scientific equipment to magnify images of distant objects so that they can discover more about the **universe**.

▲ **Early astronomers**
When astronomers first looked through telescopes, they were amazed to see so many stars. They realized that the universe was much bigger than they had thought.

▼ **Stonehenge**
Stonehenge is a circle of huge stones that was built 5,000 years ago. Many people believe that the stones were used to chart the positions of the Sun and Moon.

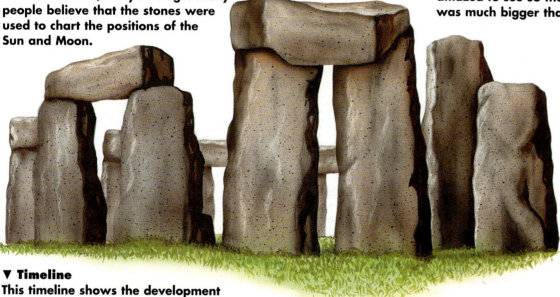

Changing views
For centuries, people believed that the Earth was at the centre of the universe. Then, in the 17th century, careful study convinced astronomers that Earth and the other **planets orbited** the Sun. Later, astronomers proved that even though the Sun is at the centre of the **solar system**, it is not at the centre of the universe. It is just one of many stars, in many **galaxies**.

▼ **Timeline**
This timeline shows the development of ideas and inventions in astronomy.

280 BC
The astronomer Aristarchus of Samos suggested correctly that the Earth circled the Sun. Most people refused to believe him.

AD 200
The Egyptian astronomer Ptolemy claimed wrongly that the Sun circled the Earth. His theory was accepted for 1,500 years.

1543
Copernicus, a Polish monk, used mathematics to show that the Earth circled the Sun. At first, his ideas were not accepted.

1608
The Dutch spectacle maker Hans Lippershey invented the first basic telescope that magnified distant objects.

1610
The Italian astronomer Galileo made observations with a telescope which led him to believe that the Earth orbited the Sun.

Modern astronomy

Today, astronomers use powerful telescopes and computers to collect and study signals from space. These machines can record the temperature of the stars and have helped to discover mysterious objects such as **black holes**. Astronomers can even measure the distance to the furthest galaxies. At the edge of the universe, almost 15 billion **light years** away, astronomers have found immensely powerful objects, called **quasars**. These objects give off an enormous amount of light, but we are still not sure what they are. They may be new galaxies being born.

BECOMING AN ASTRONOMER

With a pair of binoculars, you can look deep into space and see the mountains on the Moon and different coloured stars. If you have a star map, you can chart your way around the glittering night sky. Why not find out about joining a local or school astronomy club? But remember – always make sure you have permission from an adult to go out when it is dark.

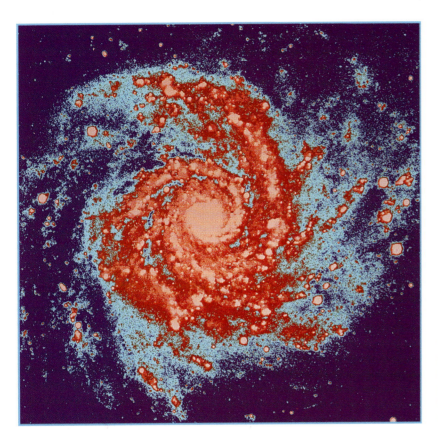

◄ False colour
Computers add colour to photographs of space. This makes the details in the picture clearer. The red area in this photograph shows the arms of a spiral galaxy.

WOW! Astronomers have found evidence of other solar systems, similar to ours, where planets orbit nearby stars.

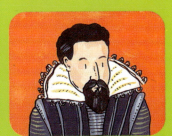

1600s
The German astronomer Johannes Kepler used the studies of Danish astronomer, Tycho Brahe, to prove that the planets circle the Sun.

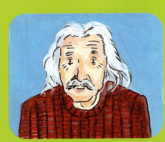

1905
Albert Einstein, the famous German scientist, proved that light travels faster than anything else in the whole universe.

1920s
Edwin Hubble discovered that there were other galaxies outside the **Milky Way**. He also claimed that the universe was expanding.

1931
Karl Jansky discovered signals from space called **radio waves**. This led to the development of radio telescopes.

1998
The **space probe**, Lunar Prospector, found ice on the Moon. If there is water on the Moon, then we may be able to live in space one day.

Telescope

Have you ever looked through a **telescope**? A telescope collects light with a mirror or a lens to make distant objects look clearer and brighter. It allows you to see objects that otherwise would remain hidden from sight. The bigger the telescope lens or mirror, the more light it captures and the more you can see.

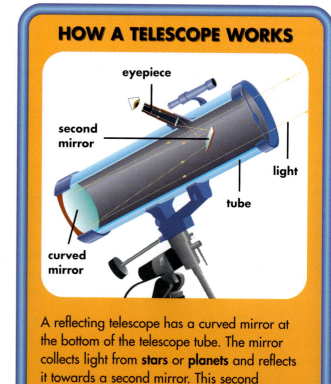

HOW A TELESCOPE WORKS

A reflecting telescope has a curved mirror at the bottom of the telescope tube. The mirror collects light from **stars** or **planets** and reflects it towards a second mirror. This second mirror directs the light into an eyepiece or a camera to show a magnified image.

Telescope history

In 1609, Galileo studied the **Moon** using a telescope with a lens. He discovered that the Moon was covered with lumps and bumps that turned out to be mountains and **craters**. Later, Isaac Newton invented a telescope that produced even clearer images than Galileo's, because it used a curved mirror instead of a lens.

◀ **Newton's telescope**
Many of today's telescopes are based on Newton's first telescope, which he designed in 1668.

Observatories

Often, **astronomers** study the sky from large telescopes built inside special houses, called **observatories**. An observatory is usually far away from city lights and pollution which can blur images of the **universe**. Sliding doors open and the telescope turns towards the sky. Usually, astronomers do not look directly through the telescope. Instead, the astronomer studies information that is passed from the telescope to a computer or a camera.

Hubble

The Hubble Space Telescope was named after the astronomer Edwin Hubble. In 1990, the telescope was launched into **orbit** round the Earth. Hubble was designed to produce crystal clear pictures of the universe. At first, the images were blurred because the main mirror was faulty. In 1993, a team of **astronauts** visited the telescope to repair the mirror. Today, Hubble works perfectly and has provided us with some amazing pictures of space.

Mirror
The mirror inside the telescope produces images that are ten times more detailed than those taken with telescopes on Earth.

Cover
This cover protects the telescope from the **Sun's** powerful rays.

Radio antenna
The antenna receives instructions from astronomers to point the telescope in different directions. It also sends images back to Earth.

Solar panel
These panels use sunlight to make electricity, which powers the telescope.

WOW!
'Is anyone out there?' This radio telescope message is on its way to the constellation Hercules. It will take 25,000 years to arrive!

Radio telescopes

In space, many objects give out **radio waves**, as well as light. Radio waves give us a different view of what is happening in space. Astronomers collect radio waves with radio telescopes. These telescopes are much bigger than telescopes that collect light. A radio telescope picks up even the weakest signals with an enormous metal dish that looks like a giant soup bowl. Powerful radio telescopes have collected information about distant stars and **galaxies** at the edge of the universe.

◀ **Arecibo**
The biggest radio telescope in the world is 305 metres (1,000 feet) wide. It is built into the crater of an extinct **volcano** in Puerto Rico, USA.

Space traveller

Until recently, few people imagined that one day humans would travel into space. This was before 1957, when a dog named Laika made the first journey into space. Since then, more than 350 human beings have followed in Laika's footsteps. These space travellers are called **astronauts**.

Early astronauts
In 1961, the Russian space traveller Yuri Gagarin became the first person to travel into space. In his small space capsule, Vostok 1, he **orbited planet** Earth in 108 minutes. Then, in 1969, the Apollo 11 spacecraft took American astronauts Neil Armstrong and Buzz Aldrin to the **Moon**. Today, the Moon is still the furthest place visited by human beings, although modern astronauts travel for longer periods and in more comfort than the first space travellers.

▼ **Apollo 11**
The footprints of the first astronauts will stay on the Moon forever because there is no wind to blow them away.

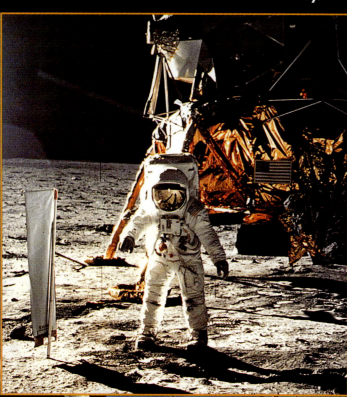

▼ An astronaut leaves the spacecraft to repair a **satellite**.

Visor
A visor protects the astronaut's eyes from the **Sun's** bright rays.

Spacesuit
When the astronaut is outside the spacecraft, a spacesuit is his life-support system.

Chest pack
The astronaut uses these controls to change the temperature inside his spacesuit.

WOW! When you travel in space, you grow 5 cm (2 in). You shrink back to normal size when you come back to Earth!

Backpack
A backpack contains an air supply which allows the astronaut to breathe in space.

Special training
All astronauts are qualified scientists, engineers or pilots, but it takes years of training before they can travel into space. Astronauts spend many hours in machines, called simulators, that imitate conditions in space. Here, astronauts prepare themselves physically for the journey and learn how to operate the equipment they will use in space. On Earth, a spacesuit weighs more than a suit of armour, but in space, astronauts feel as though they weigh nothing at all, because both the spacesuit and the astronaut are weightless.

Pocket
The spacesuit has large pockets for carrying useful tools and equipment.

▲ **Underwater training**
Astronauts practise mending machines underwater to get used to the same weightless conditions they'll find in space.

Foot restraint
The astronaut attaches his boots to foot restraints so that he does not float away!

STRANGE SPACE TRAVELLERS

Astronauts can have odd travelling companions. Mice, rats, monkeys, fish and spiders have all been into space. In 1976, two spiders, Anita and Arabella, joined a **space station** called Skylab. Scientists wanted to see if they could spin webs in space. The spiders were successful!

Rocket

A **rocket** is a powerful vehicle that launches spacecraft, such as **space probes**, **satellites** and **space shuttles**, into space. Just before the launch, an exciting countdown takes place in the launch-control building. When the rocket blasts off, blazing-hot **gases** rush out of its engines and thrust it up into the sky. The tremendous force from the gases helps the rocket to escape the pull of Earth's **gravity**.

Lift-off
A rocket is usually made of separate sections called stages. Each stage carries fuel. The stages burn up their fuel one at a time and then fall to Earth. This makes the rocket lighter, so that it can travel faster and faster. Some rockets also have booster rockets strapped to their sides which fall away just after launch. Only the cargo, called the payload, at the top of the rocket is carried all the way into space.

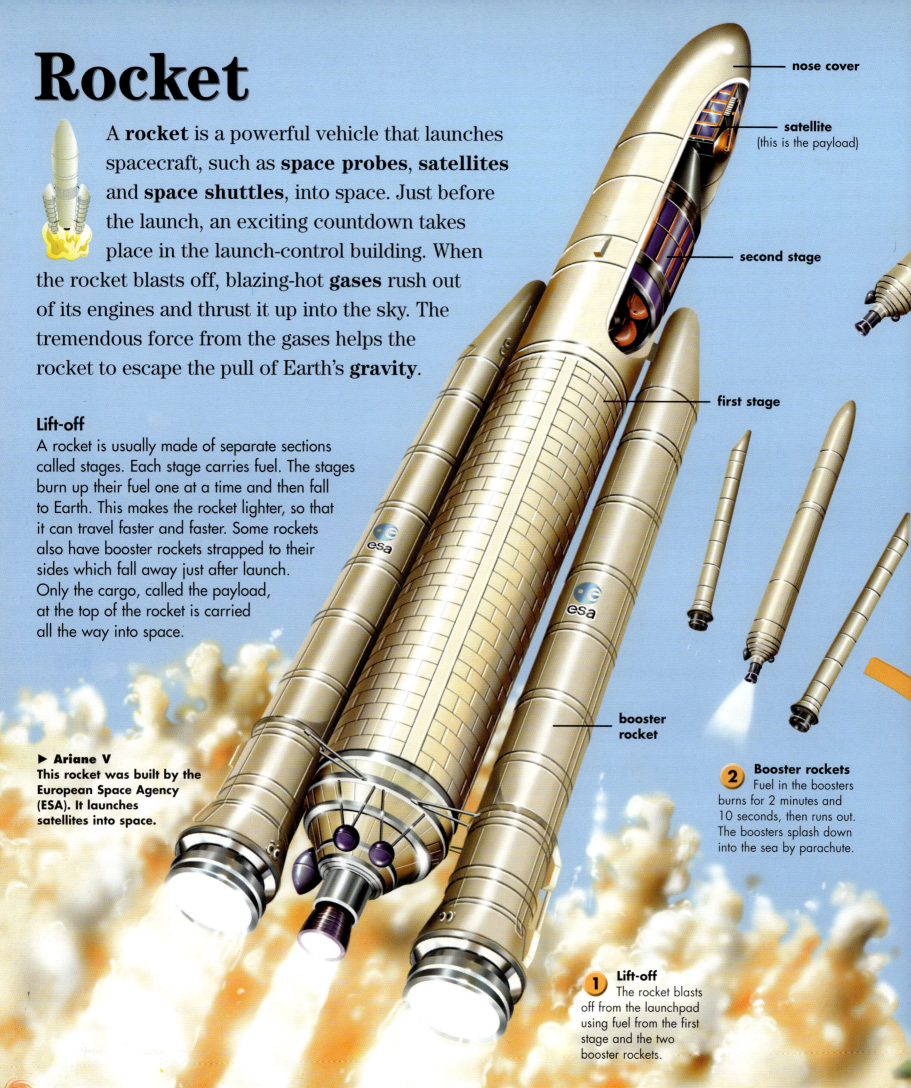

▶ **Ariane V**
This rocket was built by the European Space Agency (ESA). It launches satellites into space.

- nose cover
- satellite (this is the payload)
- second stage
- first stage
- booster rocket

1 Lift-off
The rocket blasts off from the launchpad using fuel from the first stage and the two booster rockets.

2 Booster rockets
Fuel in the boosters burns for 2 minutes and 10 seconds, then runs out. The boosters splash down into the sea by parachute.

5 Second stage
The second stage fires its engines to carry the satellite higher.

6 Satellite in space
Finally, the second stage falls away and the satellite is released into **orbit** round the Earth.

4 First stage
After 9 minutes and 50 seconds, the fuel for the first stage is used up. The first stage separates and falls to Earth.

3 Nose cover
When the rocket is about 100 km (60 mls) high, the streamlined nose cover falls away to reveal the satellite.

Saturn V
The rocket that carried three **astronauts** to the **Moon** in 1969 was called Saturn V. During the launch, the astronauts lay strapped in their seats inside the cone-shaped command module near the top of the rocket. In case of an emergency, there was a small rocket at the top of Saturn V that would catapult the module away from the main rocket to safety.

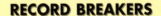

> ### RECORD BREAKERS
> **Tallest rocket**
> Saturn V is the tallest rocket ever built. At over 110 m (360 ft), it's even higher than the Statue of Liberty.
>
> **Most powerful rocket**
> The most powerful rocket ever built was the Soviet rocket, Energia. It was first launched in 1987.
>
> **First rockets**
> Gunpowder rockets have been used as fireworks and weapons for over 1,000 years.

▲ **Saturn V**
Saturn V was moved to the launchpad on a gigantic crawler with caterpillar tracks. The crawler travelled at a snail's pace.

35

Space shuttle

The **space shuttle** is the first spacecraft to travel into space, fly back to Earth and return to space again. It is the most advanced vehicle ever built. **Astronauts** and cargo travel in the main part of the shuttle, called the orbiter. The other parts are a giant fuel tank and two booster **rockets**. The fuel tank is the only part of the space shuttle that cannot be used again.

FROM LAUNCH TO LANDING

The shuttle takes off from Cape Canaveral in Florida, USA. The power from the main engines and the booster rockets pushes it into the air. You can hear a loud roar for miles around.

Shortly after launch, the boosters separate and parachute to Earth. Just before the shuttle goes into **orbit**, the empty fuel tank falls away and burns up in the Earth's **atmosphere**.

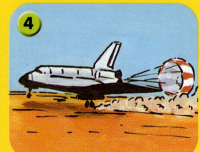

To return to Earth, the shuttle fires its engines in the opposite direction to which it is travelling. This slows the shuttle down. When it re-enters Earth's atmosphere, it glows red hot.

The shuttle usually lands back at Cape Canaveral. It touches down like an aeroplane on a runway, using its wings to balance. When the pilot brakes, a parachute opens and the shuttle glides to a stop.

Engine
The engines help to propel the shuttle into space. Once the shuttle is in orbit, the engines are switched off.

▲ **Atlantis**
There are four space shuttles – Atlantis, Columbia, Endeavour and Discovery. Atlantis made its first flight in 1984.

WOW!
In 1995, a woodpecker delayed the launch of the space shuttle Discovery. It pecked more than 75 holes in the fuel tank.

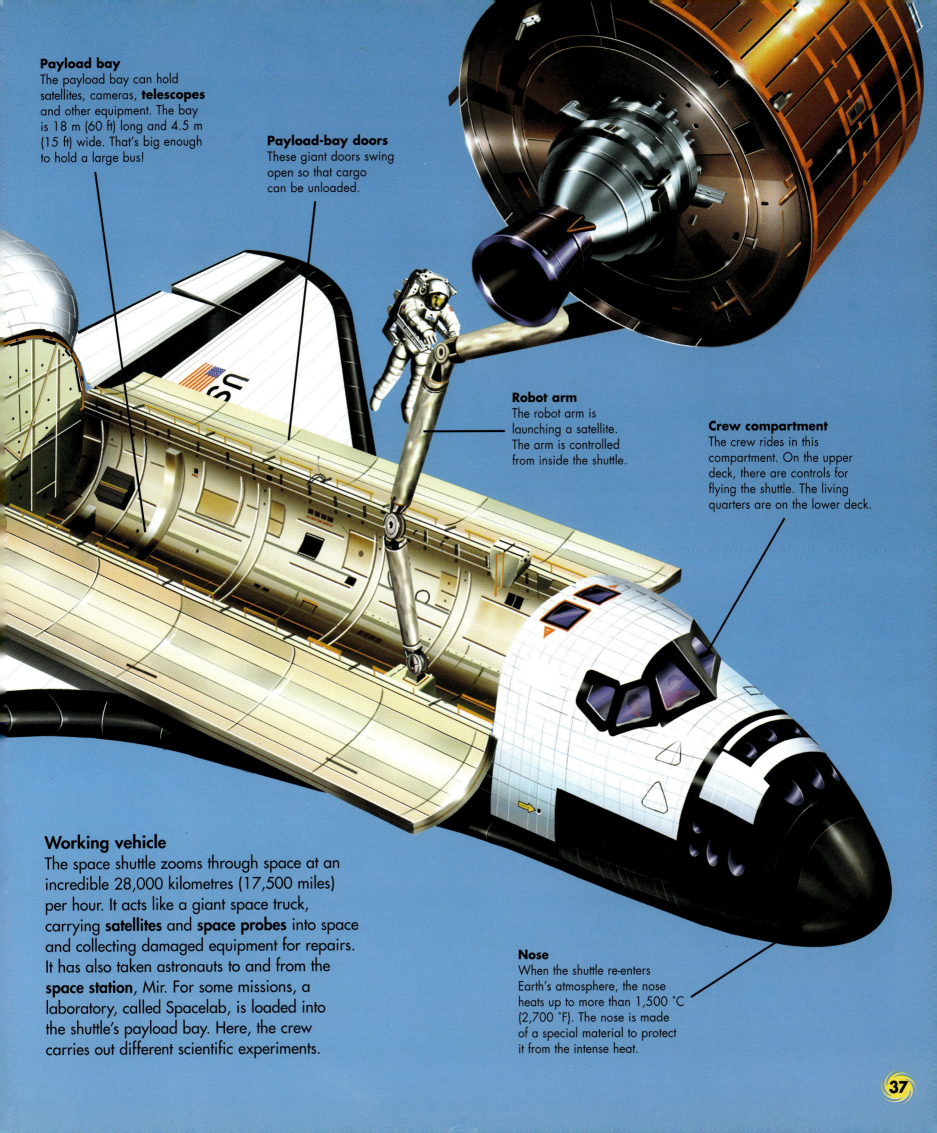

Payload bay
The payload bay can hold satellites, cameras, **telescopes** and other equipment. The bay is 18 m (60 ft) long and 4.5 m (15 ft) wide. That's big enough to hold a large bus!

Payload-bay doors
These giant doors swing open so that cargo can be unloaded.

Robot arm
The robot arm is launching a satellite. The arm is controlled from inside the shuttle.

Crew compartment
The crew rides in this compartment. On the upper deck, there are controls for flying the shuttle. The living quarters are on the lower deck.

Nose
When the shuttle re-enters Earth's atmosphere, the nose heats up to more than 1,500 °C (2,700 °F). The nose is made of a special material to protect it from the intense heat.

Working vehicle
The space shuttle zooms through space at an incredible 28,000 kilometres (17,500 miles) per hour. It acts like a giant space truck, carrying **satellites** and **space probes** into space and collecting damaged equipment for repairs. It has also taken astronauts to and from the **space station**, Mir. For some missions, a laboratory, called Spacelab, is loaded into the shuttle's payload bay. Here, the crew carries out different scientific experiments.

37

Space station

Imagine living and working in space for months at a time. That's exactly what **astronauts** do on a **space station**. A space station is a home that **orbits** Earth. It has living quarters where astronauts eat and sleep, and laboratories where they carry out experiments. On board, there is air to breathe, so members of the crew do not need to wear spacesuits.

▼ **International Space Station**
The parts for the ISS are being built on Earth. First they will be launched into space and then they will be assembled.

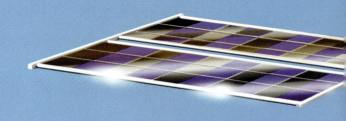

WOW! The ISS will be as long as a football pitch and weigh as much as 300 cars.

Solar panel
Solar panels will provide all the power that the space station needs. They will turn light from the **Sun** into electricity.

International Space Station (ISS)
Fourteen countries are building the International Space Station. The **space shuttle** and **rockets** will take parts of the station into space, where astronauts will fit them together, just like a giant construction kit. A robot video camera will help the astronauts to put the pieces in the right places. When the ISS is finished, it will orbit Earth every 90 minutes and travel at 3,000 kilometres (almost 1,800 miles) per hour.

Working quarters
Scientific experiments will be carried out here, in the laboratory.

Docking port
The space shuttle and other spacecraft will link to the ISS here.

Living quarters
The kitchen will have a microwave oven, so that the crew can cook meals just as they do at home on Earth.

Life on board

Weightlessness is an important part of life on board a space station. In space, astronauts push their feet into loops on the walls to stop themselves from floating around. To drink, they suck through straws. This is because liquids form blobs and drift about instead of pouring.

▲ **Living in space**
These astronauts live, sleep and eat in cramped conditions on board the Russian space station, Mir.

Mir

In 1986, the USSR launched a space station called Mir, which made huge advances in space science and paved the way for the ISS. Astronauts spent more than a year at a time living on Mir, proving that humans can survive long periods of weightlessness. Each month, spacecraft from Earth took up supplies of food and equipment.

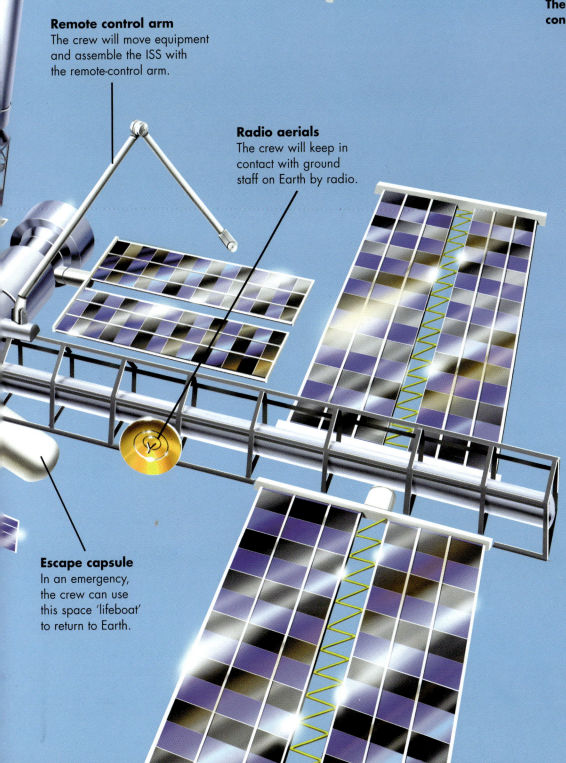

Remote control arm
The crew will move equipment and assemble the ISS with the remote-control arm.

Radio aerials
The crew will keep in contact with ground staff on Earth by radio.

Escape capsule
In an emergency, the crew can use this space 'lifeboat' to return to Earth.

▲ **Mir and the space shuttle**
In 1995, the space shuttle Atlantis docked with Mir, making a record total of ten people on board one spacecraft.

39

Space probe

A **space probe** is a robot spacecraft that flies through space collecting information about distant **planets** and **moons**. It carries video cameras which beam back up-to-the-minute pictures to scientists on Earth. Space probes have travelled to the far edge of the **solar system**, visiting all the planets except for icy Pluto.

Orbiters, landers and fly-by probes
There are three main types of space probes. A fly-by probe passes by a planet, collecting information as it travels. An orbiter probe flies closer. It **orbits** a planet, examining the **atmosphere** and surveying the surface. A lander probe touches down on a planet's surface. Some landers carry robot cars that make short trips away from the landing site to explore the surrounding area.

Mars Global Surveyor
In November 1996, an orbiter probe, called Mars Global Surveyor, set out for Mars to take pictures of the planet's atmosphere and surface. It arrived in September 1997. Since then, it has sent back amazing images of Mars, which have helped scientists to create a detailed map of the planet.

Pathfinder to Mars
In December 1996, a lander probe, called Pathfinder, was sent to Mars. When the probe reached Mars, it went straight down to the planet's surface. Just before touchdown, a parachute and four airbags opened to carry the lander safely to the ground.

◀ **Sojourner**
Inside Pathfinder, there was a tiny robot car called Sojourner. This vehicle roamed across Mars, taking photographs and testing the soil.

Galileo

In 1989, the **space shuttle** Atlantis launched Galileo. This orbiter probe took six years to fly to the planet Jupiter. During its journey, it took photographs of an **asteroid** and observed a crashing **comet**. In 1995, Galileo went into orbit around Jupiter. It recorded information about the planet's moons and dropped a smaller probe into the thick, swirling atmosphere.

IS ANYONE THERE?

Pioneer 10, a fly-by probe, has been travelling since 1972. In 1986, it flew past Pluto and left the solar system. It is carrying picture and sound messages from people on Earth to intelligent life that may exist beyond the solar system.

Cassini

Cassini, the largest fly-by space probe ever built, is the size of a bus. It was launched in 1997 and will reach Saturn in 2004. During its mission, **astronomers** are hoping to receive more than 300,000 colour pictures of Saturn's rings, atmosphere and moons. Cassini is carrying a second probe, called Huygens, which will float down by parachute to the surface of Titan, Saturn's largest moon.

Huygens
Huygens will record information about Titan's surface.

Satellite

An artificial **satellite** is a machine that circles the Earth. Satellites do many different jobs, from spotting hurricanes and studying the Earth's surface, to bouncing television programmes all the way around the world. All satellites are launched into space by **rockets** or **space shuttles**. When a satellite is in **orbit**, it is held in its path by the pull of **gravity** from the Earth.

► Comstar

Communication

A communication satellite, such as Comstar, beams radio signals from one side of the world to the other and transmits television programmes to receiving dishes fixed to people's homes. When you watch a live sporting event, such as the Olympic Games, the pictures you see are sent by a communication satellite.

Navigation

There are many navigation satellites, including Navstar, that beam signals constantly to the Earth's surface. People in ships, aeroplanes, lorries and cars with receivers can pick up the signals to work out the position of their vehicles. You can even buy hand-held navigation receivers to take with you when you go hiking in the mountains.

► Navstar

Solar panels
These panels point towards the **Sun**. They use the Sun's **energy** to power the satellite's instruments and transmitters.

Transmitters
These point towards the Earth and beam signals to receivers.

Weather

Meteosat is a weather satellite that can measure the wind and the temperature of the **atmosphere**. The satellite beams images and data back to weather forecasters on Earth who add this information to measurements taken on land. This helps forecasters to build up a picture of clouds and storms that are on the way.

▶ Meteosat

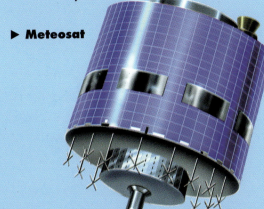

SOHO SATELLITE PROFILE
Type of satellite
Scientific satellite
Launch
December 1995, by NASA and ESA
Mission
To spend six years observing the Sun's surface and atmosphere
Orbit
1.5 million km (930,000 mls) from Earth
What SOHO has observed
Sunquakes, the solar atmosphere and 50 new **comets**, including two that crashed into the Sun

▶ SOHO

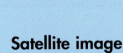

Satellite image

A satellite can 'see' normal, visible light, but it can also see invisible rays made by heat. These rays are called **infrared rays**. Satellites make images from both types of rays. When a satellite sends images back to Earth, a computer adds strong colours to the images to highlight land and sea, or places with high and low temperatures.

Earth watch

Landsat is a satellite that travels in a low orbit, scanning the Earth's surface. It uses special cameras to take pictures of the land and sea. Then the satellite beams the images back to Earth. Scientists use these images to draw maps, to study pollution and to make predictions about when earthquakes are likely to happen.

▲ **New York, USA, from space**
Landsat took this infrared image of New York. The hot spots that glow red are places, such as factories and power stations, where energy is being used.

▶ Landsat

43

Into the future

One day, in the not too distant future, there might be bases on the **Moon** and even on Mars, where people will live and work. Spacecraft might transport **astronauts** to and from space, just like commuter trains take people to work on Earth. What do you think will happen in the future?

Space station
In the future, **space stations** in **orbit** may become factories, launchpads for space missions or even human colonies.

Space plane
Reusable space planes might take people to and from orbiting space stations.

Biosphere 2
Biosphere 2 is a huge, sealed dome in the desert in Arizona, USA, where a group of eight scientists lived for two years. Inside the dome, the scientists had to be self-sufficient. They grew plants to make food and recycled their water and all their waste. This exciting experiment may help future space travellers to be able to live on other **planets**.

▶ **Moon base**
This is how scientists imagine a base on the Moon might look. Would you like to live on the Moon?

▼ **Biosphere 2**
The Biosphere dome traps the **Sun's** heat in the same way as a greenhouse. This helps the plants inside to grow.

Living quarters
Humans cannot breathe on the Moon because the **atmosphere** is too thin. Astronauts will have to live and work inside sealed modules.

Moon and Mars bases

A space mission to the Moon is planned for early in the 21st century. Astronauts may set up a permanent base there and use it as a starting point for a trip to Mars. The onward journey to Mars would take about one year. If something goes wrong on Mars, there would be no chance of rescue, so supplies and extra spacecraft will be sent to Mars in advance.

IS THERE LIFE IN OUTER SPACE?

So far, scientists haven't found a trace of life in rock and soil samples from other planets. But space is a huge place. Beyond our **solar system**, where astronauts haven't ventured yet, there might be planets where life has evolved. We just don't know!

WOW!
If you lived on the Moon, you'd feel much lighter than you do on Earth. This is because there is six times less **gravity** on the Moon than on the Earth.

Working quarters
The first explorers will mine rocks and minerals from the Moon's surface. They will study the raw materials inside the module.

Surface rovers
Astronauts will explore in air-tight vehicles with thick tyres that can move over bumpy ground. Expeditions might last for weeks at a time.

Astronauts
Outside, astronauts will need to wear spacesuits with supplies of oxygen.

45

Glossary

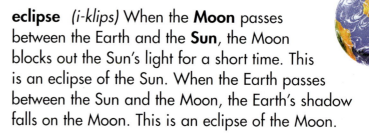

asteroid (as-te-royd) A rock that circles the **Sun**. Most asteroids travel in **orbits** that lie between the **planets** Mars and Jupiter. The biggest asteroid is more than 900 kilometres (550 miles) across.

astronaut (as-tro-nawt) A person who travels in space. Russian space travellers are known as cosmonauts.

astronomer (as-tron-o-mer) A scientist who studies the **stars** and the **planets**.

atmosphere (at-mos-fear) A layer of **gas** that surrounds a **planet**, **star** or **moon**. The atmosphere is held in place by the pull of **gravity**. Earth's atmosphere, which is called the air, is a mixture of different gases.

Big Bang The fantastic explosion that most scientists think created the **universe** about 15 **billion** years ago.

billion A number meaning one thousand million, written as 1,000,000,000.

black dwarf The cold, dark remains of a **star** that has burnt all of its **gas**.

black hole Most scientists believe that there are places in space where **gravity** is so strong that nothing, not even light, can escape once it has passed inside. A black hole forms when a **supergiant** explodes.

comet (kom-it) A ball of ice, rock and dust that travels through the **solar system**. When a comet passes close to the **Sun**, some of the ice melts. The comet develops a bright head and an enormous tail.

constellation (kon-ste-lay-shun) A group of **stars** that seems to make a pattern in the night sky. The ancient Greeks and Romans named many of the constellations.

crater A round, shallow hole in the ground which is made when a meteorite hits the surface of a **planet** or a **moon**.

eclipse (i-klips) When the **Moon** passes between the Earth and the **Sun**, the Moon blocks out the Sun's light for a short time. This is an eclipse of the Sun. When the Earth passes between the Sun and the Moon, the Earth's shadow falls on the Moon. This is an eclipse of the Moon.

elliptical (i-lip-ti-kal) Almost round, like a circle, or long and thin, like a squashed oval shape.

energy The force that makes things move or work. Energy can be felt as heat, or seen as light. A **star** gives out huge quantities of energy in the form of heat and light.

galaxy A vast **star** 'city' that is made of **billions** of stars and **nebulae**. There are four main kinds of galaxies: a spiral galaxy, a barred spiral galaxy, an **elliptical** galaxy and an irregular galaxy.

gas A substance, such as air, that has no shape and can be felt only when it moves.

gravity The force that holds **planets** and **moons** in their **orbits** round the **Sun**. The same force pulls you towards Earth's surface and gives you weight.

infrared rays (in-fra-red) A type of ray, like a ray of light, that people cannot see. All objects give off infrared rays. **Satellites** can see these invisible rays and use them to make images.

light year A measure of distance used by **astronomers**. A light year is the distance that light travels through space in one year (9.5 million million kilometres or 5.9 million million miles).

mass The amount of material that a body contains. The mass of a **star** is the amount of **gas** it contains.

meteoroid (mee-tee-or-oyd) A rock spinning in space. When a meteoroid enters Earth's **atmosphere**, it burns up, leaving a bright trail in the sky. This is called a meteor. When a meteoroid lands on Earth without burning up, we call it a meteorite.

Milky Way The name for our **galaxy**. On a clear night, you can see the Milky Way as a bright band of light stretching across the night sky. The **Sun** is one of **billions** of **stars** in the Milky Way.

moon A natural, rocky object in space that moves in **orbit** round a **planet**. A moon is always smaller than its planet. The Earth has one moon, whereas Saturn has at least 18.

nebula (ne-byu-la) A huge cloud of dust and **gas** in a **galaxy**, where **stars** form.

neutron star (nyu-tron star) The remains of a **supergiant** after a **supernova** explosion. A teaspoonful of neutron **star** would weigh as much as a mountain.

nuclear fusion (nyu-clee-er few-zhun) **Stars** contain a **gas** called hydrogen. When hydrogen becomes extremely hot, it splits into tiny particles. The particles smash into each other, making a new gas called helium. This creates a huge amount of **energy** that makes stars glow.

observatory (ob-zer-va-tree) Domed buildings in which **astronomers** keep and use their **telescopes**.

orbit The curved path of an object as it travels in space round a larger object. A **planet** orbits, or circles, a **star** such as the **Sun**, while a **satellite** orbits a planet.

planet A large, round object in space, such as the Earth, that **orbits** the **Sun** or another **star**.

quasar (kway-zar) A **gas** cloud coming together to form a young **galaxy**. Quasars are the furthest objects from Earth in the **universe** and also the brightest.

radio wave An invisible wave that travels through air and space, carrying information that can be made into sounds or pictures. Radio **telescopes** can detect natural radio waves created by **stars** and **galaxies**.

red giant A **star**, towards the end of its life, that has cooled down and grown to many times its original size.

rocket A vehicle that can carry **astronauts** or **satellites** into space. A rocket has powerful engines that thrust it into space.

satellite (sat-uh-lite) An object that travels round a **moon** or a **planet**. Moons are natural satellites of planets. Artificial satellites are machines that are launched by **rocket** or **space shuttle** and orbit the Earth.

solar system The **Sun** and all the bodies that travel round it, such as **planets**, **moons**, **comets** and **asteroids**.

space probe A robot spacecraft that is sent to explore the **solar system**.

space shuttle A reusable spacecraft for carrying **astronauts** into space. A space shuttle is launched like a **rocket** and flies back to Earth on wings like an aeroplane.

space station A large structure, built in space, that **orbits** the Earth. A space station is a place where **astronauts** live and work. In the future, space stations may be used to launch spacecraft.

star An enormous ball of hot **gas** in space, which gives out huge quantities of heat and light.

Sun The nearest **star** to Earth. The Sun is the star around which the Earth and the other **planets** travel in their **orbits**.

supergiant An enormous red or blue **star**. A supergiant forms when a massive star cools and expands towards the end of its life. A supergiant usually ends its life as a **supernova**.

supernova (su-per-no-va) The explosion of a **supergiant** at the end of its life. All that is left after the explosion is a **neutron star** or a **black hole**.

telescope (tel-e-skope) A scientific instrument for collecting and focusing light or **radio waves**. With the help of large telescopes, scientists can study **galaxies** in the most distant parts of the **universe**.

universe All of space and everything that exists within it.

volcano (vol-kay-no) A hole in the surface of a **moon** or **planet** through which **gas** and molten rock, called lava, escape. The lava builds up into a cone-shaped mountain.

white dwarf The cold remains of a dying **star** after it has been a **red giant**.

Index

Aldrin, Buzz 32
Andromeda Galaxy 27
Arecibo Telescope 31
Aristarchus of Samos 28
Armstrong, Neil 32
asteroid 6, 13, 20, 21, 41
asteroid belt 7, 21
astrolabe 25
astronaut 31, 32, 33, 35, 36, 37, 38, 39, 44, 45
astronomer 11, 15, 18, 20, 21, 23, 24, 27, 28, 29, 30, 31, 41
astronomy 28, 29
atmosphere 4, 8, 9, 10, 11, 12, 13, 15, 20, 21, 36, 37, 40, 41, 43, 45

Big Bang 4
Biosphere 2 44
black dwarf 22
black hole 4, 23, 29
Brahe, Tycho 29

Callisto 16
Caloris Basin 10
Cape Canaveral 36
Charon 19
comet 20, 21, 41, 43
command module 35
constellation 24, 25, 31
Copernicus 28
crater 10, 11, 13, 14, 15, 21, 30, 31

Deimos 15

Earth 4, 5, 6, 7, 8, 9, 10, 11, 12, 13, 14, 15, 16, 17, 18, 19, 20, 21, 22, 23, 25, 27, 28, 31, 32, 33, 34, 35, 36, 37, 38, 39, 40, 41, 42, 43, 44, 45
Einstein, Albert 29
Enceladus 7
Europa 16
European Space Agency (ESA) 34, 43

Gagarin, Yuri 32
galaxy 4, 5, 6, 26, 27, 28, 29, 31
Galileo 28, 30
Ganymede 16
gravity 6, 23, 34, 42, 45

Halley, Edmond 20
Halley's comet 20
Herschel, William 18
Hubble, Edwin 29, 31
Hubble Space Telescope 5, 31

Io 16

Jansky, Karl 29
Jupiter 5, 7, 16, 17, 21, 41

Kepler, Johannes 29

Laika the dog 32
light year 5, 23, 27, 29
Lippershey, Hans 28

Magellanic Clouds 27
Mars 7, 14, 15, 21, 40, 44, 45
Mercury 7, 10
meteor 20, 21
meteorite 21
meteoroid 20, 21
Milky Way 26, 27, 29
Miranda 18
moon 4, 6, 7, 9, 10, 11, 12, 13, 15, 16, 17, 18, 19, 28, 29, 30, 32, 35, 40, 41, 44, 45

NASA 43
nebula 4, 5, 22
Neptune 6, 17, 18, 19
neutron star 23
Newton, Isaac 6, 30
North Star 25
nuclear fusion 9

Observatory 30
Olympus Mons 14

Payload 34, 37
Phobos 15
planet 4, 5, 6, 7, 8, 10, 11, 12, 14, 15, 16, 18, 19, 21, 28, 29, 40, 41, 44, 45
Pluto 6, 18, 19, 40, 41
Ptolemy 28

Quasar 29

Radio telescope 29, 31
radio wave 29, 31
red giant 22
Rigel 5
rocket 34, 35, 36, 38, 42; Ariane V 34, 35; Energia 35; Saturn V 35; Vostok 1 32

Satellite 32, 34, 35, 37, 42, 43; Comstar 42; Landsat 43; Meteosat 43; Navstar 42; SOHO 43
Saturn 5, 7, 16, 17, 41
Saturn's rings 17, 41
scientist 4, 6, 15, 21, 33, 40, 43, 44, 45

simulator 33
Sirius 25
Sojourner 40
solar eclipse 9
solar system 4, 6, 7, 11, 12, 16, 19, 21, 27, 28, 29, 40, 45
space probe 11, 19, 34, 37, 40, 41; Cassini 41; Galileo 41; Huygens 41; Lunar Prospector 29; Magellan 11; Mars Global Surveyor 40; Pathfinder 40; Pioneer 10 41; Viking Lander 15; Voyager 17; Voyager 2 19
space shuttle 5, 34, 36, 37, 38, 39, 41, 42; Atlantis 36, 37, 39, 41; Columbia 36; Discovery 36; Endeavour 36
space station 37, 38, 39, 44; International Space Station (ISS) 38, 39; Mir 37, 39; Skylab 33
space traveller *see* astronaut
Spacelab 37
spacesuit 32, 33, 38, 45
star 4, 5, 6, 8, 22, 23, 24, 25, 26, 27, 28, 29, 31
Stonehenge 28
Sun 4, 6, 7, 8, 9, 10, 11, 12, 13, 14, 15, 16, 17, 18, 19, 20, 22, 23, 25, 27, 28, 29, 31, 32, 38, 42, 43
supergiant 23
supernova 23

Telescope 5, 15, 26, 27, 28, 29, 30, 31, 37
Titan 41
Triton 19

Universe 4, 6, 26, 27, 28, 29, 30
Uranus 6, 17, 18

Venus 7, 10, 11

Weightlessness 33, 39
white dwarf 22

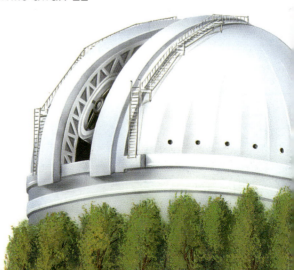

48